WITHDRAWN

SEA MONSTERS

by Melissa Higgins

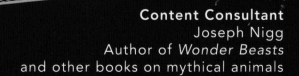

Content Consultant
Joseph Nigg
Author of *Wonder Beasts*
and other books on mythical animals

CORE
LIBRARY

Published by ABDO Publishing Company, PO Box 398166, Minneapolis, MN 55439. Copyright © 2014 by Abdo Consulting Group, Inc. International copyrights reserved in all countries. No part of this book may be reproduced in any form without written permission from the publisher. The Core Library™ is a trademark and logo of ABDO Publishing Company.

Printed in the United States of America,
North Mankato, Minnesota
092013
012014

♲ THIS BOOK CONTAINS AT LEAST 10% RECYCLED MATERIALS.

Editor: Lauren Coss
Series Designer: Becky Daum

Library of Congress Cataloging-in-Publication Data
Higgins, Melissa, 1953-
  Sea monsters / by Melissa Higgins.
    pages cm. -- (Creatures of legend)
  Includes bibliographical references and index.
  ISBN 978-1-62403-152-6
1. Sea monsters--Juvenile literature. 2. Cryptozoology--Juvenile literature.
I. Title.
  QL89.2.S4H54 2014
  001.944--dc23
                        2013027270

CONTENTS

DANGER BELOW!

Elliott helped his father push their small fishing boat into the lake. It was a cold morning in the Scottish Highlands. Elliott rubbed his arms for warmth. He was also trying to calm his nerves. Ever since he was a young boy, his mother had warned him of creatures that lived in Loch Ness, a Scottish lake. He shook his head. He was grown now. Legends were nothing to be afraid of.

People have reported seeing mysterious creatures in oceans, lakes, and rivers for thousands of years.

"C'mon, then," his father said. He held the boat still for Elliott. "Let's get going."

The boat teetered as Elliott climbed in. His dad pushed them off. They made their way toward the middle of Loch Ness. The water was murky and dark. Elliott could see only a few inches deep. He shivered, remembering his mother's warnings. Who knew what creatures lurked beneath their boat?

Elliott and his father threw out their fishing lines. An eerie quiet settled over the loch. Then Elliott heard a splashing sound. A few yards to his right, a curved object sped through the water. The object rose. Elliott saw an oval-shaped eye. Then he spotted a broad, horse-shaped head.

"Father!" he yelled.

"I see it," his father whispered, his voice shaking.

They watched in amazement as the monster's long neck extended. It rose six feet (1.8 m) above the water. Behind its neck, three humps broke the surface. Elliott guessed the last hump extended 40 feet (12 m) back from the animal's neck. Its skin was rough and dark. Large waves from the creature's movements reached their boat. The waves spun the boat around. By the time Elliott and his father were in a position to see it again, the monster had disappeared. The only remaining evidence were the waves lapping against their boat.

Nessie

The Loch Ness Monster, nicknamed "Nessie," is one of the most famous water creatures. The story of Elliott and his father is not true. But it closely matches some accounts of Nessie sightings over the years. Since the 1930s there have been thousands of recorded sightings of the serpent.

Loch Ness

Loch is the Scottish word for "lake." Loch Ness is one mile (1.6 km) wide and 24 miles (39 km) long. It is very cold and deep. In places the lake is more than 700 feet (213 m) deep. Loch Ness is one of the largest bodies of fresh water in Europe. Peat seeping from the surrounding land makes the loch murky and dark. The darkness only adds to the loch's mystery.

Colonel Robert Wilson's 1934 photo drew visitors to the mysterious Loch Ness. People hoped to see the monster for themselves.

Strange creatures had been reported at Loch Ness since the 500s CE. But the first modern sighting took place in 1933. In April of that year, hotel manager Aldie Mackay reported seeing a huge animal in Loch Ness. She thought it looked like a whale. In 1934 Colonel Robert Wilson took a strange photograph at Loch Ness. The photo appeared to be of a creature sticking its head and long neck out of the lake. The picture fired up the public's imagination. But the photo turned out to be a hoax. Wilson had actually photographed a miniature dinosaur attached to a toy submarine. However, people didn't stop believing in the monster.

The Search Continues

Legends of creatures living in lakes, rivers, and oceans have been around since people first began exploring bodies of water. As sailors set out on long ocean voyages, they caught glimpses of strange animals. These creatures were often whales or giant squid. But they often looked like

The Vast Ocean

The sea is enormous. It's no wonder there are so many legends of creatures hiding in its depths. Water covers more than 70 percent of the earth's surface. According to the US National Oceanic and Atmospheric Administration, only 5 percent of the oceans have been explored. This means 95 percent of the oceans have not been seen by human eyes. Scientists estimate that up to 1 million ocean plant and animal species are yet to be discovered.

A group of cryptozoologists search for Storsjöodjuret, a monster said to live in Lake Storsjön in northern Sweden.

nothing witnesses had ever seen before. They looked like monsters.

Unknown species of animals are known as cryptids. Cryptozoologists are people who study animals that have not been proven to exist. Many

FURTHER EVIDENCE

Chapter One discusses creatures from the deep and whether or not they are real. What was a main point of this chapter? What pieces of evidence support this point? Check out the Web site at the link below. Does the information on this Web site support the main point in Chapter One? Write a few sentences using new information from the Web site as evidence to support the main point in this chapter.

Unknown Marine Species
www.mycorelibrary.com/sea-monsters

cryptozoologists are also biologists, zoologists, or naturalists. They often use scientific methods. But cryptozoology is not a recognized science.

No one has yet found pieces of bone, tissue, or other physical evidence proving sea monsters are real. Still, cryptozoologists around the world are looking for evidence of sea monsters. Until these people find proof, the Loch Ness Monster and other sea monsters will remain legends.

Butirum

Bremē

Hordero

Sudero

FARE

B

A

Eclea

Mulse

C   Moachus

Stremb

A

Amora sperma
Ceti

O   P

Ziphius

D

D   E

300.

CHAPTER TWO

PHYSICAL FEATURES

Hundreds of years ago, sea monsters came in all shapes and sizes. Some were multi-armed, many-headed beasts. Other creatures were thought to be so massive they could be mistaken for islands. Maps from the 1500s showed drawings of frightening pig-fish, bat-winged sea dragons, and devil fish. These were creatures sailors feared when they began exploring the world's lakes and oceans.

Old maps show some of the strange monsters sailors believed to be swimming in oceans around the globe.

A Living Fossil

The coelacanth is a fish five feet (1.5 m) long with huge eyes and thick blue scales. Scientists once thought the fish had been extinct for 70 million years. But in 1938, one was caught in the net of a South African fishing boat. Since then, more coelacanths have been found. The discovery has encouraged sea-monster believers. They wonder what other amazing creatures are waiting to be discovered in the depths of the sea.

As science began to take the place of superstition, most sea creatures were explained. They turned out to be giant octopuses, giant squid, or whales. Sharks, seals, flying fish, otters, and large eels were also mistaken for monsters. But in some people's minds, one category of sea monster still defied logical explanation: the serpent.

Serpents

One of the most famous recorded sightings of a sea serpent was by British sea captain Peter M'Quhae. In 1848 his ship, *Daedalus*, was sailing off the southwest coast of Africa. A huge snake-like creature moved

The coelacanth was thought to be extinct until it was discovered in 1938.

swiftly toward his ship. The captain and his crew watched in amazement. According to M'Quhae's report, the creature held its head four feet (1.2 m) above the water. M'Quhae estimated the creature was more than 60 feet (18 m) long.

During the 1800s and 1900s, people reported thousands of such sightings of sea and lake serpents. Believers and spotters included sailors, policemen, and people from all backgrounds. In the mid-1900s, cryptozoologist Bernard Heuvelmans gathered information from more than 500 different sightings.

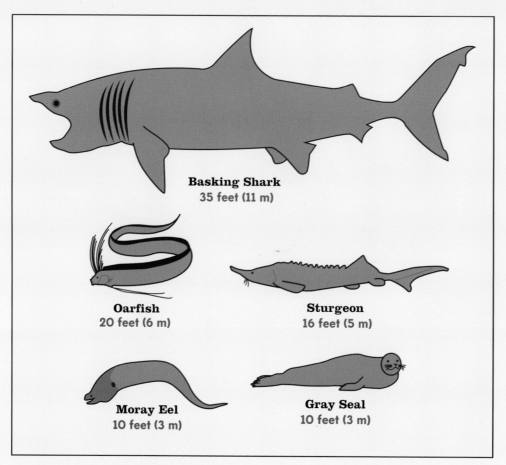

Basking Shark
35 feet (11 m)

Oarfish
20 feet (6 m)

Sturgeon
16 feet (5 m)

Moray Eel
10 feet (3 m)

Gray Seal
10 feet (3 m)

Real-Life Sea Monsters?

The illustrations above show different animals that have been mistaken for sea or lake serpents. Compare these animals with the descriptions of sea monsters mentioned in this chapter. What features of the animals above might cause them to be confused with monsters? Can you think of any other real animals that could be confused with a sea monster?

From those descriptions, he grouped serpents into

nine categories: long-necked, merhorse, many-

humped, many-finned, super-otter, super-eel, marine

saurian, father-of-all-the-turtles, and yellow-belly.
Since then, other cryptozoologists have come up with
their own groupings.

What Are They?

Some cryptozoologists believe serpents might be a
species of animal still completely unknown. Others
believe sea serpents might be an animal once
believed to be extinct. Cryptozoologists consider the
zeuglodon, an extinct
whale, a likely suspect
for serpent sightings.
The plesiosaur, an extinct
reptile, is another strong
possibility.

Some people who
report sea serpents know
they haven't seen the
monsters. These people
are often lying or playing
a joke. They might do

Plesiosaurs

Plesiosaurs were long-necked
reptiles. They lived in the
ocean more than 80 million
years ago. Plesiosaurs had
broad flat bodies and short
tails. They had fins that they
flapped to move through
the water. Plesiosaurs have
been extinct for millions of
years. Scientists learn about
plesiosaurs by studying
fossils.

Many cryptozoologists believe the Loch Ness Monster and other water cryptids are actually extinct dinosaurs called plesiosaurs.

this to gain media attention. Other sighters mistake one object for another. The serpent they see might actually be a floating log, an overturned boat, or seaweed. Other reported serpents might be known fish or sea mammals. People have confused sturgeons, giant eels, giant otters, seals, sharks, and oarfish with sea serpents.

In spite of a lack of evidence, the mystery of unknown water creatures living in lakes and oceans continues to enchant believers. But the first sea monsters were not enchanting in the least.

Captain Peter M'Quhae of the ship *Daedalus* provided this description to a London newspaper of the creature he and his crew saw in 1848:

> *The diameter of the serpent was about fifteen or sixteen inches behind the head, which was, without any doubt, that of a snake; and it was never, during the twenty minutes that it continued in sight of our glasses, once below the surface of the water; its colour a dark brown, with yellowish white about the throat. It had no fins, but something like the mane of a horse, or rather a bunch of seaweed, washed about its back.*
>
> Source: Alfred T. Story. "The Sea-Serpent." The Strand Magazine July–Sept. 1895: 163. Print.

Consider Your Audience

Carefully read this passage. M'Quhae's description of the creature was written for an 1800s audience. How might you rewrite this passage for a modern audience? Write a blog post conveying the information in this passage to a new audience, such as your friends, teachers, or siblings. How is your approach different from M'Quhae's description? What do you think M'Quhae might have seen?

CHAPTER THREE

THE HISTORY OF SEA MONSTERS

An octopus is a very unusual-looking sea creature. It has a rounded head and long sucker-covered arms. Some early fishermen and sailors who spied octopuses in their nets thought they were monsters. In fact, most legends of sea monsters began with very real fish and whales.

Octopuses may have been the real animals behind some sea monster legends.

Early Legends

Around 800 or 900 BCE, the Greek poet Homer wrote a long poem called the *Odyssey*. In the *Odyssey*, he describes a creature called Scylla. Scylla is a terrifying monster with many feet, necks, and heads. The creature resembles a human octopus.

In the Middle Ages, from the 400s to the 1400s CE, came the legend of the Island Beast. This was a whale-like monster. The Island Beast was so huge that sailors might have mistaken it for an island. A similar creature began appearing in Norse legends around 1000 CE. It was called the kraken.

The Kraken

Scandinavian explorers first described an enormous sea creature known as the kraken in approximately 1000 CE. In 1752 Scandinavian bishop Erik Ludvigsen Pontoppidan described the kraken in a book on the natural history of Norway. Pontoppidan's kraken was one and a half miles (2.4 km) around. It had a flexible back that was said to look like several small islands.

The kraken was known to sink ships with its many arms.

In the mid-1800s, scientists began wondering if the giant squid was the source of the kraken tale. At the time, a number of giant squid were washing ashore. At 55 feet (16.8 m), one was longer than a school bus. In 1896 an enormous octopus washed onto a Florida beach. The tentacles alone were 32 feet (9.8 m) long. Today most people accept that these real giant sea creatures were the source of the early kraken legends. Few people still believe in the kraken.

More Sightings

Giant squid may also be the source of other sea monster legends, including sea serpents. These

In 2012 scientists were able to capture video footage of a real monster, the giant squid. Dead giant squid had been washing up on beaches around the world for hundreds of years. But scientists had yet to film a live giant squid in its natural habitat. A Japanese-led team of scientists hoped to change this. The team used a small submarine to dive deep into the ocean. After approximately 100 dives, they finally spotted their prize. The 10-foot (3-m) long monster was swimming at nearly 3,000 feet (900 m) below the surface. Eventually the footage was shown on a television special for the Discovery Channel.

enormous snake-like creatures have long been a part of sailing lore. In 1734 a Norwegian missionary named Hans Egede provided the first reliable description of a sea serpent. Egede had been sailing off the coast of Greenland. In his book *Description of Greenland*, he reported seeing a "very terrible sea monster." The creature raised its head as high as the ship's main sail. The animal had broad flippers. It was covered with hard, wrinkled skin. Its body was shaped like a snake.

A live giant squid was filmed in its habitat for the first time in 2012.

Today many skeptics believe Egede may have actually spotted a giant squid. From a distance, the tentacles may have looked like the serpent's head and tail.

In 1817 almost 100 people reported seeing a snake-shaped creature swimming swiftly near Gloucester, Massachusetts. It was seen again and again over the next several days. The reports

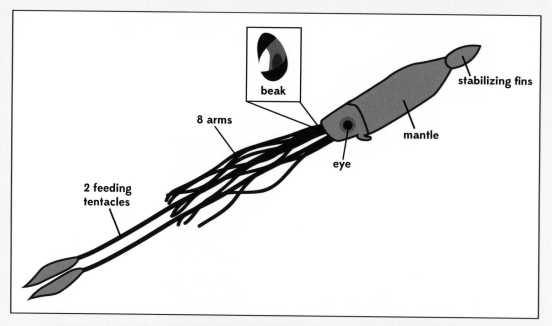

8 arms

2 feeding
tentacles

beak

stabilizing fins

mantle

eye

Anatomy of a Giant Squid

Giant squid are strange-looking and mysterious creatures. Many humans have mistaken them for krakens and other sea monsters. This diagram shows the different parts that make up a giant squid. Look closely at the diagram. Then reread some of the sea monster legends covered in this chapter. What are some of the squid's features that might be mistaken for parts of a sea monster? Why?

continued until the 1960s. Scientists still aren't sure what Gloucester residents spotted off the coast.

In 1905 two naturalists saw a similar creature near Brazil. They reported seeing a huge turtle-like head rise seven to eight feet (2.1–2.4 m) out of the water. The beast was dark brown on top. The lower part of its body was white.

The Mystery Continues

In the late 1800s and early 1900s, ships powered by coal engines became more and more common. These ships were much faster than sailing ships. Reported sightings of sea serpents became fewer with the arrival of these engine-powered ships.

According to some cryptozoologists, the creatures dislike the sound of ships' engines. As a result, they avoid shipping lanes. Sightings of serpents and other sea monsters have since decreased. But they certainly did not end. In many ways, the mystery has only grown.

A Serpent Hoax

In 1845 Albert Koch took advantage of the public's interest in sea serpents. He gathered bones from whales and other animals. Then he formed them into the shape of a snake-like skeleton 114 feet (34.7 m) long. He claimed it was a giant sea serpent. He charged people to see his monster. A scientist who saw the display in New York discovered his hoax. Koch then took his skeleton on a tour of Europe. He eventually sold his monster to the king of Prussia. It ended up in Berlin's Royal Anatomical Museum in Germany.

MORE SIGHTINGS

Sea monsters aren't spotted only in oceans. People have also claimed to see strange creatures in lakes, rivers, and swamps. Legendary creatures have been spotted in bodies of water around the world, including in Scandinavia, Ireland, Siberia, Argentina, and Africa.

Ogopogo is a monster said to live in Lake Okanagan in British Columbia, Canada.

Other Water Creatures

Some myths of sea creatures reflect a fear of the water at a time when many people were unable to swim. In Scotland, *selkies* were seals that could turn themselves into humans. *Kelpies* were water horses that carried their riders into the ocean, where they drowned. In Japan, *kappa* were human-like creatures with scaly skin that drowned people. In Zambia, the Tonga people have told legends about a creature with the torso of a snake and the head of a fish. Known as the Nyaminyami River God, the creature is said to live in the Zambezi River.

Lake Monsters

The Loch Ness Monster is the most famous lake serpent. However, many lakes have claimed resident monsters. Loch Morar in Scotland also boasts a monster called Morag. Lake Morar sits 70 miles (110 km) from Loch Ness. There is no road around the lake, making it very isolated. Some tales describe Morag as a female, mermaid-like creature. Today Morag is usually described as being dark colored and snake-like with several large humps.

One of the most famous North American legends is of a monster known as Champ. Champ is rumored to swim the deep, cold waters of Lake Champlain. Lake Champlain sits on the border of New York and Vermont. The lake is more than 100 miles (160 km) long. It is up to 400 feet (120 m) deep in places. Iroquois legends of a serpent living in the lake date back to well before European settlers arrived in the area. But sightings have been most common in the last 200 years. Thousands of Champ sightings have been reported since 1873. The beast is most often described as a

Mermaids

Mermaids aren't exactly monsters. But the half-human, half-fish beings have appeared in many cultures for a very long time. A mermaid-like creature was drawn on a cave wall 30,000 years ago. Mermaids also appeared in Greek myths. In some Asian cultures, mermaids were thought to be the wives of sea dragons. In the 1700s, some royal families in Europe claimed to be descended from mermaids. However, no one has ever found evidence of a real mermaid.

Mermaids are one of the most well-known mythical sea creatures. Mermaid legends go back thousands of years.

dark, snake-like creature more than 100 feet (30 m) long.

A serpent in Lake Okanagan in British Columbia, Canada, was given the name Ogopogo. European settlers in the area were so terrified of the creature

EXPLORE ONLINE

Chapter Four touches on the legends of several lake monsters, including Lake Champlain's Champ. The Web site below also discusses Champ. As you know, every source is different. How is the information given at the Web site different from the information in this chapter? What information is the same? How do the two sources present information differently? What can you learn from this Web site?

The Legend of Champ
www.mycorelibrary.com/sea-monsters

that they patrolled the lakeshore at night. Ogopogo is described as being a serpent with large eyes and dark skin.

There is little evidence supporting the existence of such monsters. Most scientists believe people who claim to have seen these creatures are actually spotting other things. They may be seeing anything from floating logs to large fish. But despite the lack of proof, the mysterious legends continue.

CHAPTER FIVE

SEA MONSTERS TODAY

Cryptozoologists may never prove the existence of sea monsters. But these legendary creatures are still popular subjects of television shows, movies, and books.

Sea Monsters in the Media

Some terrifying sea monsters have found their way into writers' imaginations. Herman Melville's classic *Moby Dick* was first published in 1851. In this novel,

Sea monsters have made their way into many books and movies. In Jules Verne's story *20,000 Leagues under the Sea,* sailors on a submarine are attacked by a giant squid.

Sea-Monster Movies

Many notable films feature scary creatures from the deep:

- *Jaws*, 1975: A monstrous great white shark menaces a seaside community.
- *The Abyss*, 1989: Divers come face-to-face with an alien aquatic species.
- *Leviathan*, 1989: A mutating creature with tentacles roams a deserted ship.
- *The Beast*, 1996: A giant squid terrorizes a small seaside town.
- *Deep Rising*, 1998: Cruise-ship passengers face off against an angry octopus creature.
- *Mega Shark vs. Giant Octopus*, 2009: Two sea creatures battle one another off the California coast.

Captain Ahab goes up against a ship-destroying white whale. Jules Verne, another well-known author, first published *20,000 Leagues under the Sea* in 1870. In Verne's story, Captain Nemo of the submarine *Nautilus* faces off against a giant squid.

Moviemakers also love the idea of creatures lurking in the inky depths. Some of the best-loved sea-monster movies were made in the 1950s. In the 1953 film *The Beast from 20,000 Fathoms*, nuclear weapons testing creates

In the film The Water Horse: Legend of the Deep, a young boy befriends a mysterious creature that lives in a Scottish lake.

a dinosaur-like monster that terrorizes New York City. In 1954's *Godzilla*, a similar monster threatens Tokyo, Japan.

The Loch Ness Monster has a few movies of its own. In the 1996 film *Loch Ness*, an American scientist is sent to Scotland to prove the existence of the lake's monster. In the 2007 movie *The Water Horse: Legend of the Deep*, a boy finds a mysterious egg at the loch. A strange serpent-like creature hatches from the egg.

A number of documentaries have also been made about Loch Ness. PBS aired *The Beast of Loch Ness* in 1999. More recently, *National Geographic* produced *The Truth Behind: The Loch Ness Monster* in 2012. In both films, scientists try to get to the bottom of the mystery surrounding the Loch Ness Monster. They have little success.

High-Tech Searches

Few scientists accept that sea monsters are real. But people around the world continue to believe in the mysterious creatures. That may be why the search for them continues. Since the fuzzy photo taken in 1934, searches for the Loch Ness Monster have

Monsters for Profit?

Dr. Charles Paxton, a Scottish ecologist, sifted through 800 eyewitness accounts of the Loch Ness Monster. He found that a large number of reports were from hotel and café owners near Loch Ness. These included hotel manager Aldie Mackay. Paxton's research suggests that those who reported sightings were trying to boost tourism. Loch Ness tourism brings in more than $1.5 million to the area every year.

A scientist uses sonar equipment to search for the Loch Ness Monster during a 1989 investigation.

gone high-tech. In 1987 Operation Deepscan used sonar equipment to try to find the monster. Sonar equipment uses sound waves to detect underwater objects. Over a period of two days, 24 boats searched the loch. Their equipment made contact with a large unidentified object at a depth of 600 feet (180 m). Scientists still aren't sure what the object was.

By 2013 the quest for Nessie had reached the Internet. A number of video cameras were placed around Loch Ness. Video from the cameras could be viewed online 24 hours a day. The Nessie-cam Web

Water monsters have captured the imaginations of people around the world. In 2009 a model of a monster was placed in a lake in Minneapolis, Minnesota.

site has averaged 33,000 hits per month. But even using the eyesight of millions of people around the world, no real evidence has been uncovered.

Why do people continue looking for creatures that science tells them should not exist? As one Loch Ness Monster skeptic told an interviewer in 2013, "I think people find the idea of a twenty-first century monster . . . irresistibly romantic."

Alastair Boyd claimed to see the Loch Ness Monster in 1979. In 1994 he discovered the famous 1934 photo of the monster had been faked. In the 1999 PBS documentary *The Beast of Loch Ness*, Boyd tells an interviewer his views on the monster's existence:

> I'm so convinced of the reality of these creatures that I would actually stake my life on their existence. I trust my eyesight . . . I used to make my living teaching people how to observe, and I know that the thing I saw was not a log or an otter or a wave, or anything like that. It was a large animal. It came heaving out of the water, something like a whale. I mean, the part that was actually on the surface when it stopped rolling through was at least 20 feet long. It was totally extraordinary. It's the most amazing thing I've ever seen in my life, and if I could afford to spend the rest of my life looking for another glimpse of it, I would.
>
> Source: Stephen Lyons. "The Legend of Loch Ness." NOVA. WGBH, 1999. Web. Accessed April 25, 2013.

Changing Minds

In the passage above, Boyd describes his belief in the Loch Ness Monster. After reading this book, do you believe in sea monsters? Write a short essay trying to convince someone that sea monsters are real or don't exist. Make sure to use evidence to support your opinions.

Kraken

Seas near Norway and Iceland

Legends dating back to the 1000s CE say this gigantic creature was one and a half miles (2.4 km) around and had octopus-like arms.

Cadborosaurus (Caddy)

Cadboro Bay, British Columbia, Canada

Caddy is a serpent estimated to be 40 to 70 feet (12–21 m) long. Sightings have been reported along the British Columbia coast since the 1800s. There have been 300 recorded Caddy sightings over the past 200 years.

Kiao and Shan

China

In Chinese myths dating back to ancient times, the Kiao is part dragon and part serpent. It lives in lakes. The serpent Shan lives in the sea. It has ears, a red mane, and horns. European sailors reportedly saw a sea serpent near Asia in 1876.

Nahuelito

Nahuel Huapi Lake, Argentina

Nahuelito has been described as looking like a serpent or a plesiosaur about 100 feet (30 m) long. Most sightings are in the summer, when the lake is calm. Some people have claimed the monster emerges onto land.

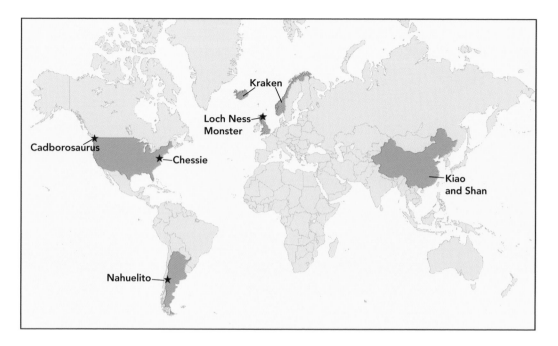

- Kraken
- Loch Ness Monster
- Cadborosaurus
- Chessie
- Kiao and Shan
- Nahuelito

Loch Ness Monster

Loch Ness, Northern Scotland

The most famous of all lake monsters, the Loch Ness Monster has had thousands of sightings since the 500s CE. The beast is said to have a horse-shaped or lizard-like head on a long neck. Its back is humped.

Chessie

Chesapeake Bay, Maryland, United States

Chessie has been described as black and snake-like with a football-shaped head. Some people believe the monster may actually be a large eel or a giant anaconda snake.

Dig Deeper

After reading this book, what questions do you still have about sea monsters? Do you want to learn more about the Loch Ness Monster? Or how sea monster legends began? Write down one or two questions that can guide you in doing research. With an adult's help, find a few reliable sources that can help answer your questions. Write a few sentences about how you did your research and what you learned from it.

Another View

This book has a lot of information about sea monsters. As you know, every source is different. Ask a librarian or another adult to help you find another source about sea monsters. Write a short essay comparing and contrasting the new source's point of view with that of this book's author. What is the point of view of each author? How are they similar and why? How are they different and why?

Say What?

Studying books that involve biology and zoology can mean learning a lot of new vocabulary. Find five words in this book that you've never heard before. Use a dictionary to find out what they mean. Then write the meanings in your own words, and use each word in a new sentence.

You Are There

This book discusses modern sea-monster sightings. Imagine you're standing on the edge of a lake and notice something strange in the water. You think it might be a sea serpent! How do you feel? Who might you tell about your sighting?

GLOSSARY

cryptozoologist
a person who studies creatures that have not been proven to exist by modern science

ecologist
a scientist who studies the relationships between living things and their environments

eyewitness
someone who sees something firsthand

hoax
a trick

loch
lake

missionary
a person who is sent somewhere to teach about religion or perform service work

naturalist
expert in natural history

peat
material formed in soggy ground

skeptic
a person who is doubtful of something's existence

sonar
a device that sends out underwater sound waves to detect the location of underwater objects

superstition
belief in something that's not real

zoologist
a scientist who studies animals

LEARN MORE

Books

Hamilton, S. L. *Beasts*. Edina, MN: ABDO, 2011.

Newquist, H. P. *Here There Be Monsters: The Legendary Kraken and the Giant Squid*. Boston: Houghton Mifflin Books for Children, 2010.

Schach, David. *The Loch Ness Monster*. Minneapolis: Bellwether, 2011.

Web Links

To learn more about sea monsters, visit ABDO Publishing Company online at **www.abdopublishing.com**. Web sites about sea monsters are featured on our Book Links page. These links are routinely monitored and updated to provide the most current information available.

Visit **www.mycorelibrary.com** for free additional tools for teachers and students.

INDEX

ABOUT THE AUTHOR

Melissa Higgins is the author of more than 30 books for children and young adults. She also writes short stories and novels. Before pursuing a writing career, Higgins worked as a counselor in schools and private practice.